AMAZING ATHLETES

AN ALL-STAR LOOK AT CANADA'S PARALYMPIANS

Written by Marie-Claude Ouellet
Translated by Phyllis Aronoff and Howard Scott

Owlkids Books

Words followed by an asterisk* are defined in the glossary.

Owlkids Books acknowledges the financial support of the Canada Council for the Arts, the Ontario Arts Council, the Government of Canada through the Canada Book Fund (CBF) and the Government of Ontario through the Ontario Creates Book Initiative for our publishing activities.

Published in Canada by
Owlkids Books Inc.
1 Eglinton Avenue East
Toronto, ON M4P 3A1

Published in the United States by
Owlkids Books Inc.
1700 Fourth Street
Berkeley, CA 94710

Library of Congress Control Number: 2021931892
Library and Archives Canada Cataloguing in Publication
Title: Amazing athletes : an all-star look at Canada's Paralympians / written by Marie-Claude Ouellet ; illustrated by Jacques Goldstyn ; translated by Phyllis Aronoff and Howard Scott.
Other titles: Des athlètes époustouflants. English
Names: Ouellet, Marie-Claude (Biologist), author. | Goldstyn, Jacques, illustrator. | Aronoff, Phyllis, 1945- translator. | Scott, Howard, 1952- translator.
Description: Translation of: Des athlètes époustouflants, au cœur des Jeux paralympiques.
Identifiers: Canadiana 20210153229 | ISBN 9781771474856 (hardcover)
Subjects: LCSH: Paralympic Games—Juvenile literature. | LCSH: Sports for people with disabilities—Canada—Juvenile literature. | LCSH: Athletes with disabilities—Canada—Juvenile literature.
Classification: LCC GV722.5.S64 O9413 2021 | DDC j796.04/560971—dc23

Photos (T = top, B = bottom, R = right, L = left)
© **International Paralympic Committee:** p. 4 (logo); © **Canadian Paralympic Committee:** p. 6T, 26B, Matthew Murnaghan (p. 1, 5B, 6B, 7L, 13, 16, 17, 22B, 27, 28, 37), Phillip MacCallum (p. 4, 30B), Matthew Manor (p. 7R, 15T, 19), Dave Holland (p. 8, 10T, 15B, 31, 34, 39, 43B, 44, 46, 47), Scott Grant (p. 9, 11T, 14, 18, 20, 21, 23, 25, 36, 38, 42, 43T), Benoit Pelosse (p. 12, 22T, 33), Angela Burger (p. 24, 26T), unknown (p. 26B), Mike Ridewood (p. 29), Bob Frid (p. 30T), Jean-Baptiste Benavent (p. 32, 35T), Brittany Gawley (p. 35B), Dan Galbraith (p. 40), Daniel Marcotte (p. 41); **Public Domain:** p. 5T; **Wheelchair Basketball Canada:** p. 45; **World ParaVolley:** p. 11B

ONTARIO ARTS COUNCIL
CONSEIL DES ARTS DE L'ONTARIO
an Ontario government agency
un organisme du gouvernement de l'Ontario

 Canada Council for the Arts   Conseil des Arts du Canada

Canadä

Manufactured in Altona, MB, Canada, in April 2021 by Friesens   Job #275031

A   B   C   D   E   F   G

OWL kids Publisher of Chirp, Chickadee and OWL
www.owlkidsbooks.com | Owlkids Books is a division of  bayard canada

 Canadian Paralympic Committee
100-85 Plymouth St., Ottawa (Ontario) Canada K1S 3E2   info@paralympic.ca paralympic.ca

TABLE OF CONTENTS

THE PARALYMPIC GAMES

The Paralympic Games bring together the best high-performance athletes with disabilities from many countries. They are organized by the International Paralympic Committee (IPC), which was founded in 1989.

This is the Paralympic symbol. It represents the motto of the IPC: "Spirit in Motion." Its colours—red, blue, and green—are the hues most often found on the flags of the world's countries.

The origin of *Paralympic*

The word *Paralympic* is formed from the prefix *para*, meaning "beside" or "alongside," and the word *Olympic*—because the Paralympic Games are held "alongside" the Olympic Games.

Since 1988, they have taken place about two weeks after the Olympic Games, in the same sports facilities.

Fair and equitable competition

Para sports are a range of sporting activities for athletes with various types of physical, visual, or intellectual disabilities. It is important to ensure that athletes competing against each other have comparable abilities. This guarantees that the athletes' success is determined by their skills, physical fitness, endurance, concentration, and strategic capabilities, rather than by the extent of their impairment. Each athlete is therefore placed in a category. This system is similar to the weight classes in sports such as judo or boxing.

The father of the Paralympic Games

The Paralympic Games owe their start to Sir Ludwig Guttmann, a German-born doctor who in 1948 organized a competition near London for veterans wounded in the two world wars. Sir Ludwig envisaged these games growing into an international event for athletes with disabilities. His dream became a reality in 1960, in Rome, with what's now considered the first-ever Paralympic Games. There, athletes competed in 8 different sports (now there are 28!)—and a movement had begun. Today the Paralympic Games are held every two years, with summer sports alternating with the winter ones.

SPORTS INCLUDED IN THE PARALYMPIC GAMES

SUMMER PARA SPORTS

Boccia
Football 5-a-side
Goalball
Para archery
Para athletics
Para badminton
Para canoe
Para cycling

Para equestrian
Para judo
Para powerlifting
Para rowing
Para swimming
Para table tennis
Para taekwondo

Para triathlon
Shooting Para sport
Sitting volleyball
Wheelchair basketball
Wheelchair fencing
Wheelchair rugby
Wheelchair tennis

WINTER PARA SPORTS

Para alpine skiing
Para ice hockey
Para nordic skiing (includes Para biathlon and Para cross-country skiing)
Para snowboard
Wheelchair curling

Gaining popularity ...

With each competition, the Paralympic Games have brought together more and more athletes from all over the world. In 1960, there were 400 participants from 23 countries. In 2016, there were more than 4,300 from 160 countries!

... and getting more buzz

For many years, the spotlight was only on the Olympic Games. That changed in Sydney, in 2000, when the organizers were determined to give the Paralympic Games equal footing. The following statistics show how the Paralympic Games have been gaining more attention in recent years:

- In 2012, Canadian television devoted seven hours of airtime to the summer Paralympic Games in London, focusing mainly on Para athletics and Para swimming. In 2016, the airtime increased to 300 hours and included a wider variety of sports, such as Boccia and Goalball.

- The Paralympic Winter Games have often drawn less attention because they include fewer sports. However, media recognition has increased substantially in recent years. In Canada, the number of people watching, listening to, or reading about the Paralympic Games (television, radio, newspapers, the web, and social media) went from three million in 2010 to two billion in 2018. Coverage on the Internet and on social media has boosted the visibility of the Paralympic Games. Deservedly so!

Canada and the Paralympic Games, a love story!

Canadians have every reason to be proud of our Paralympic athletes. Our country does well in the Paralympic Games, with competitors* routinely qualifying for the majority of summer and winter sports. From 1976 to 2008, Canada placed in the top seven countries in numbers of medals. However, with the increase in participating countries and athletes, the level of competition has become a lot higher. As a result, Canada slipped to 14th place in the 2016 Games. The athletes and the Canadian Paralympic Committee have redoubled their efforts to once again reach the top ... Stay tuned!

HOST CITIES

Summer Games

Year	Host City	Country
2021	Tokyo	Japan
2016	Rio de Janeiro	Brazil
2012	London	United Kingdom
2008	Beijing	China
2004	Athens	Greece
2000	Sydney	Australia
1996	Atlanta	United States
1992	Barcelona	Spain
1988	Seoul	South Korea
1984	Stoke Mandeville	United Kingdom
1984	New York City	United States
1980	Arnhem	Netherlands
1976	Toronto	Canada
1972	Heidelberg	Germany
1968	Tel Aviv	Israel
1964	Tokyo	Japan
1960	Rome	Italy

Winter Games

Year	Host City	Country
2022	Beijing	China
2018	PyeongChang	South Korea
2014	Sochi	Russia
2010	Vancouver	Canada
2006	Turin	Italy
2002	Salt Lake City	United States
1998	Nagano	Japan
1994	Lillehammer	Norway
1992	Tignes–Albertville	France
1988	Innsbruck	Austria
1984	Innsbruck	Austria
1980	Geilo	Norway
1976	Örnsköldsvik	Sweden

JAMOI ANDERSON

Sport: Sitting volleyball

Date of birth: November 13, 1985

Birthplace: Toronto, Ontario

Inspired by: Kobe Bryant, five-time NBA (National Basketball Association) champion

As a child, Jamoi Anderson enjoyed playing baseball, soccer, football, and especially basketball. He joined a basketball team as a teen and became an excellent player. But after a serious illness which resulted in him losing part of his leg, Jamoi took up Sitting volleyball. His progress in the sport was amazing, and just a few months after he began playing, he was recruited by the national team. In 2015, in his first international competition, he experienced one of the highlights of his career.

"I was competing in the Parapan American Games* in Toronto, and I was excited about playing on Canadian soil. In the match against Colombia for third place, I scored the winning point, which earned my team the bronze medal. It was great to win that victory in front of my family, my friends, and the Canadian fans!" he says.

A TOUGH ROAD

When he was 23, Jamoi was hospitalized with a viral infection. He spent a month unconscious, in a coma. The medical treatment he received saved his life, but his left leg had to be amputated* below the knee. After the operation, he went through a long period of rehabilitation.

"I was very motivated to recover my muscle strength and learn to walk with a prosthesis.* I wanted to manage on my own in my everyday activities. Today I'm very comfortable with my abilities, doing things I enjoyed even before my amputation. My recreation nowadays is often with able-bodied individuals, so I can say I'm right back where I was," he explains. "My multi-sport prosthetic allows me to run, jump, and quickly change direction."

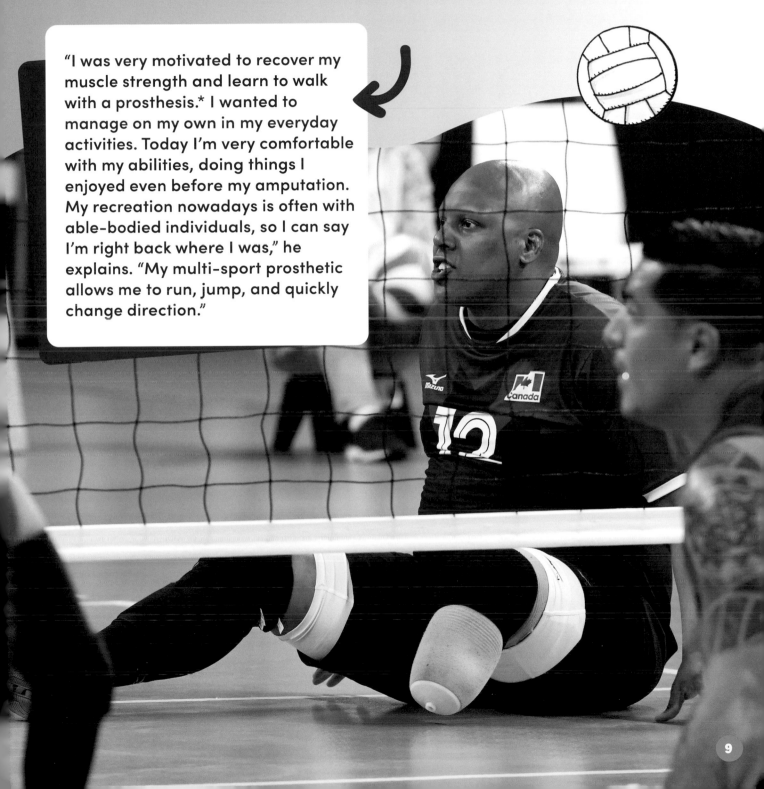

Getting back to competitive sport

In 2011, after his period of rehab, Jamoi was looking for a sport suited to his new condition.

"A friend who knew how much I missed competition suggested I try Sitting volleyball. I hesitated at first, wondering what was the point of working so hard to learn to stand again if I was going to play sitting down," he says.

Jamoi quickly realized that he *liked* playing sitting down—and he was good at it! He became a formidable front-row player, known for his powerful, precise shots.

SITTING VOLLEYBALL

Sitting volleyball became an official sport at the 1980 Paralympic Games in Arnhem, Netherlands. Elite players have great muscle strength in their torsos and arms, sharp reflexes, good balance, and amazing endurance.

Main differences from traditional volleyball

- The players sit on the floor.

- The court is smaller, and the net is lower.

- Blocking or attacking an opponent's serve is allowed.

- Players of traditional volleyball say that Sitting volleyball is more demanding.

AN ATHLETE AND HUMANITARIAN

In 2018, Jamoi founded LIVEable Society, an organization dedicated to encouraging people to adopt positive attitudes and healthy lifestyles while respecting each other's differences.

"For me, it's important to treat others the way I would like to be treated."

The quiet strength of Jolan Wong

Jolan Wong played soccer and volleyball as a child and dreamed of becoming an Olympic athlete. But at the age of 13, she had her right leg amputated as a result of bone cancer. The young Albertan thought her dream was no longer possible. However, five years later, she started playing Sitting volleyball and was quickly recruited by Team Canada. The team won the bronze medal at the 2015 Parapan American Games, which earned them a spot at the Rio Paralympic Games. It was the first time a Canadian Sitting volleyball team qualified for the Paralympic Games, and Jolan had the honour of being the team captain.

BILLY BRIDGES

Sport: Para ice hockey

Date of birth:
March 22, 1984

Birthplace: Summerside,
Prince Edward Island

Inspired by: His wife, Sami
Jo Small, an Olympic athlete
and former goaltender
for the Canadian women's
hockey team

Billy Bridges has always been extremely proud of playing hockey, Canada's national winter sport. This talented athlete was selected for the Canadian Para ice hockey team when he was only 14. At that time, in 1998, the average age of his teammates was 45.

After playing for 22 years, Billy has become one of the best Para ice hockey players in the world. With his team, he has won four World Championships. And he has competed in five consecutive Paralympic Winter Games, from 2002 to 2018.

"I'm very happy my team won a gold medal at the 2006 Games," Billy says. "But I also got a lot of satisfaction from taking the silver medal in 2018. I worked so hard for that!"

A HUGE HOCKEY FAN

Billy was born with a spinal malformation called spina bifida. He uses crutches and occasionally a wheelchair for mobility. As a child, he took part in any sport that could be practised with crutches, including soccer and skateboarding. He liked watching hockey on TV and he admired Guy Lafleur, the famous player for the Montreal Canadiens. When he was 12, Billy discovered Para ice hockey and fell in love with it.

PARA ICE HOCKEY

Formerly called sledge hockey, this sport became an official event at the Lillehammer 1994 Paralympic Winter Games. Each player sits on a double-blade sledge* and uses sticks with two different ends: a spike end to propel the sledge across the ice and a blade end to shoot the puck. The main challenge of the sport is using the arms both to move around and to control the puck.

A team player

Billy plays centre, and he's famous for his slapshot. The speed of his shots—which he accomplishes using just one arm—has been measured at nearly 130 km/h. What incredible power!

"What I enjoy most is the team spirit that bonds my friends and me. It's a tough, very physical sport, with fights and checking," Billy explains.

Competing in the Paralympic Games is always an intense and memorable experience.

"It's thrilling to parade in front of tens of thousands of cheering spectators at the Opening Ceremony," Billy says. "As for the Closing Ceremony, the participants experience it differently depending on their performance. For some, it's filled with satisfaction, and for others, sadness. It's very moving to share these moments with athletes from all over the world. It unites us at a deep level."

YOU GET OUT WHAT YOU PUT IN

Billy believes firmly that you can achieve what you want if you put in the necessary energy. Nothing is handed to you on a silver platter! Right now, he's working hard to prepare for the Beijing Paralympic Winter Games in 2022. In addition to training 20 to 30 hours a week, he follows a very strict nutrition program.

OUTSTANDING GOALIE DOMINIC LAROCQUE

Quebecker Dominic Larocque has been on the Canadian Para ice hockey team since 2010. A veteran of the war in Afghanistan, he discovered the sport thanks to a program for wounded Canadian soldiers. He first showed his talent as a forward, helping his team win a bronze medal at the Sochi Paralympic Winter Games in 2014, but after that, he switched to goalie and has never looked back. In 2017, Dominic and Team Canada won gold at the World Para Ice Hockey Championships, and the following year, silver at the PyeongChang Paralympic Winter Games. Goaltending suits him!

INA FORREST

Sport: Wheelchair curling

Date of birth: May 25, 1962

Birthplace: Fort St. John, British Columbia

Inspired by: Her parents, who are strong and loving, and who always encouraged her to persevere*

Growing up, Ina Forrest was very athletic. But at the age of 21, she was in a car accident and lost the use of her legs. Ina had to use a wheelchair for mobility and she gave up sports. During the next 16 years, she continued her university studies, married, and started a family. Things changed for her in 2004, when she happened to meet a wheelchair user who suggested she take up curling at her local curling club. Surprised to learn that Wheelchair curling existed, Ina gave it a try. It was love at first throw! The 42-year-old discovered she had talent and realized how much she had missed competitive sport.

WHEELCHAIR CURLING

This relatively new sport has been practised in Europe since 1998 and in Canada since 2001. Today, it is popular in some 20 countries. It made its debut as a medal sport at the 2006 Paralympic Winter Games in Turin, Italy. To excel at it, you need good upper body strength, since the stone weighs close to 20 kg. Wheelchair curling also requires precision, concentration, strategy, and strong team spirit.

Main differences from traditional curling

- Seated in a wheelchair, the player throws the stone using a delivery stick.

- A teammate holds the chair from behind to keep it from moving.

- In traditional curling, players called sweepers sweep the ice to change the trajectory of the stone and increase the distance it slides. But in Wheelchair curling, there are no sweepers. Everything depends on the thrower, who has to throw with great accuracy.

SPECTACULAR PROGRESS

Two weeks after starting to play, Ina was selected for the British Columbia team. Two months later, the team won a silver medal at the Canadian Wheelchair Curling Championship. In 2007, Ina joined Team Canada and received her first athlete's jacket in the mail.

"I'll always remember how proud I felt when I put it on. It gave me the shivers!" she says.

And when the team won a gold medal in Vancouver in 2010, she was overjoyed.

"That victory was very dear to me because it happened in my native province. It was great to celebrate with my family and friends. I've never felt so proud to be Canadian!"

Ina's winning streak continued with a gold medal at the 2014 Paralympic Winter Games and a bronze at the 2018 Games.

A stellar record

Ina Forrest has won numerous medals during her time as a Wheelchair curler. But this athlete isn't resting on her laurels.

"I keep on training very hard because the quality of play is improving year after year everywhere in the world. I really want to compete in the Beijing Winter Games in 2022."

THE REMARKABLE SONJA GAUDET

Sonja Gaudet is the most decorated Wheelchair curler in the world, which means she's won more medals than anyone else in her sport. She won gold three times at the Paralympic Winter Games (in 2006, 2010, and 2014). Add to that her three gold medals at the World Wheelchair Curling Championship (in 2009, 2011, and 2013), and it's a truly extraordinary haul. Sonja has been using a wheelchair since the age of 31, after a fall from a horse. Six years later, she discovered a passion and a natural talent for Wheelchair curling and joined Team Canada. She retired from competition in 2016.

BENOÎT HUOT

Sport: Para swimming

Date of birth:
January 24, 1984

Birthplace: Longueuil,
Quebec

Inspired by: Philippe Gagnon,
Paralympic athlete and
public speaker

Sports analysts agree that Benoît Huot is a model of discipline, perseverance, and determination.

"I'm pigheaded, too!" he adds with a laugh.

These qualities have served Benoît well, because he's one of the most decorated Canadian Paralympic athletes. In five Paralympic Games, he won 20 medals. He also won 32 medals at six World Championships, setting more than 60 world records in his category.

The key to success

To become a high-performance athlete, you have to put in a huge amount of time and effort.

"I used to spend about 25 hours a week training in the pool and the gym. That's equivalent to the amount of time a student spends in class. It didn't give me much chance to have fun and see my friends. I also followed a strict diet ... no chips or chocolate!" he says.

In fact, Benoît was such a fast, powerful swimmer that he earned the nickname "the shark." A very nice shark, of course!

Finding Para swimming

In 1997, Benoît watched the Canada Summer Games on television and witnessed the victory of Philippe Gagnon, another swimmer with a club foot. He realized then that he, too, could compete in Para swimming. He had a string of successes and, at age 16, he won six medals at his first Paralympic Games, in Sydney, Australia.

A passion born in childhood

As a child, Benoît liked playing hockey and baseball. But he realized he would never become a champion because of his club foot. His right leg, which was less flexible and muscular than his left, hindered his performance. It was frustrating because he was very competitive. But when he was eight, he discovered swimming, which filled him with a sense of well-being and joy. Thanks to the buoyancy of the water, Benoît could swim like a fish. At 10, he was competing alongside swimmers without disabilities.

Learning experiences

From 1998 to 2006, Benoît Huot dominated his sport. He seemed unbeatable. But the arrival of a fierce competitor, the Brazilian swimmer André Brasil, changed everything. At the Beijing Games in 2008, Benoît was weakened by a virus and he was unseated by André. He came home from those Games angry and disappointed. He even lost the desire to swim. This failure led him to change his training methods.

"Instead of aiming to be the champion at all costs, I tried to rediscover the joy of swimming, the joy I had when I was eight."

The change in attitude worked for him, and at the London Paralympic Games in 2012, Benoît won three medals, including a gold.

In 2015, Benoît went through another difficult period. For almost six months, he had a feeling of panic and suffocation whenever he put his head under water. He was experiencing performance anxiety. With the help of psychologists, he was able to control it and start training again. The following year, he ended his career in style, winning a bronze medal at the Paralympic Games in Rio.

An active retirement

Although he's now retired, Benoît is still very busy. Besides being involved in projects to help make sports accessible to all children, he also works to increase recognition for Para sports.

"I dream of a day when the public considers a Paralympic medal just as valuable as an Olympic medal. To achieve that, we have to increase the visibility of Paralympic athletes."

AURÉLIE RIVARD, QUEEN OF THE RIO GAMES

Like her mentor Benoît Huot, the Para swimmer Aurélie Rivard is an exceptional athlete. In addition to holding many world records, she won a silver medal at the 2012 Paralympic Games and four medals (three gold and one silver) at the 2016 Games. Born with a slight malformation of her left hand, Aurélie was not bothered by her impairment until she was bullied by other students in high school. She took refuge in the swimming pool, where she felt at home. Thanks to sports, Aurélie gained the confidence to stand up to her bullies. And in 2012, when she came back to school with her medal, everyone cheered.

ALISON LEVINE

Sport: Boccia

Date of birth:
May 11, 1990

Birthplace: Montreal,
Quebec

Inspired by: Her mom,
who is also her sport
assistant, and Marco
Dispaltro, who taught
her to play Boccia

Alison Levine is extremely
determined and can adapt to
almost any situation.

"When you have a disability or a
degenerative* disease, you have
to be able to find solutions as your
condition changes," she says.

Alison has done this brilliantly, practising
various sports at different times in her life.
At 12, she learned that she had a form of
muscular dystrophy. She decided to sign
up for therapeutic* horseback riding
lessons to improve her balance and
muscle strength, and she won several
competitions against riders without
disabilities. When she was no longer able
to ride a horse, she switched to
Wheelchair basketball, then Para ice
hockey and Wheelchair rugby.

"Rugby was my favourite sport because it
let me go wild!" Alison says.

A GIFT FOR THE GAME

In 2012, Alison met Boccia player Marco Dispaltro, who was looking for new prospects. She threw a few balls and realized she had talent. Three weeks later, she joined the Quebec team, and three months after that, the Canadian team. Such a rapid rise was amazing, since it usually takes about a decade to become a good Boccia player.

"Doing other competitive sports enabled me to develop precision, concentration, resilience,* and a positive attitude," Alison explains. "In Boccia, you have less than ten seconds to analyze the situation and take your turn. It's stressful, but I love it!"

BOCCIA

Boccia is a sport of precision and strategy, played with coloured leather balls. The goal of the game is to throw the balls as close as possible to a white ball, called a jack. It is a mixed-gender sport and can be played by individuals, pairs, or teams. Boccia was first featured at the 1984 Paralympic Games in New York.

A WINNING DECISION

In 2015, after seeing other athletes throw the ball underhand rather than overhand, Alison changed her own technique... and she started to climb in the rankings. By 2019, she was number one in the world in her category—the first woman ever to reach that position.

"I hope [my achievement] will encourage more girls to play Boccia. We're just as good as the boys!" she says.

Training to win

Because of her fragile health, Alison only trains in the gym every other day. That gives her body time to recover. On her rest days, she does physiotherapy,* trains on a stationary hand bicycle, prepares mentally for competition, and studies Boccia videos.

Alison lives in an apartment with Ghia, a service dog trained by the Mira Foundation. The dog assists Alison in many ways, including picking up things she's dropped, helping her take off her coat and socks, and pressing the buttons to open automatic doors.

Seizing opportunities

Alison appreciates the experiences she's had thanks to Boccia, including travelling all over the world.

"I make the most of every moment. It's important to have fun in everything you do. There are always ups and downs in life. You have to focus on the ups and accept the downs. I'm lucky to practise a sport I love so much! My biggest dream is to win a gold medal at the Paralympic Games."

PAUL GAUTHIER'S WORLD-CLASS CAREER

Boccia has four classes of players, based on the extent of their disabilities (how their arms and legs function, whether they can grasp the ball, etc.). Some players propel the ball with their hands or feet, while others, such as Canadian champion Paul Gauthier, use a ramp and head pointer (a rod attached to a helmet to allow for hands-free ball release). Gauthier, who is from Vancouver, has competed in five Paralympic Games and won four medals, including a gold in individual competition and a bronze in pairs in Athens. An impressive haul!

RICHARD PETER

Sports: Wheelchair basketball and Para badminton

Date of birth: September 10, 1972

Birthplace: Duncan, British Columbia

Inspired by: Athletes who perform at a higher level than he does

Originally from Duncan, on Vancouver Island, Richard Peter is a member of the Cowichan Tribes. He feels that the support of his family and his community have played a crucial role in his athletic successes.

"I'm very proud of belonging to the Cowichan Tribes, and it's an honour to represent them," he says.

Richard was on the Canadian Wheelchair basketball team for 18 years. He had an illustrious career, competing in five Paralympic Games. His team won three gold medals (in 2000, 2004, and 2012) and a silver (in 2008).

In 2012, Richard received a National Aboriginal Achievement Award for his athletic accomplishments. That year, at the age of 40, he retired from basketball. In 2017, he returned to competitive sport in Para badminton, and he won a bronze medal in doubles at the Lima 2019 Parapan American Games.

LEADING BY EXAMPLE

Richard has been using a wheelchair since he was four years old, when he lost the use of his legs after being hit by a bus. As a boy, he tried a lot of different wheelchair sports, including track and field, tennis, and racquetball. At 15, he fell in love with basketball. He soon became a star player who was highly valued by his coaches and teammates. Everyone praised his concentration, determination, and dynamism. He is a true role model.

WHEELCHAIR BASKETBALL

Wheelchair basketball was one of eight sports on the program of the first Paralympic Games, in 1960. It's a lot like traditional basketball—the height of the baskets and the ball used are the same—but in Wheelchair basketball, the player who has the ball is not allowed to touch his or her wheels more than twice without dribbling, and players are not allowed to touch the playing surface with their feet.

Paying it forward

In recognition of those who helped him realize his dream, Richard makes it a priority to give back to his community. He has organized camps enabling young people with disabilities to discover Para sports. And currently, he is an ambassador for the BC Wheelchair Sports Association's Indigenous Bridging the Gap Program. Through these endeavours, he passes on values such as co-operation, perseverance, and determination, while emphasizing the importance of having fun. What a wonderful mentor!

PATRICK ANDERSON OWNS THE COURT

Patrick Anderson (in Team Canada jersey, left) has been called the best Wheelchair basketball player in the world, and one of the best to ever play the game. He discovered the sport when he was 10 years old, a year after being hit by a car and having his legs amputated below the knee.

"At a wheelchair sports camp, I tried basketball, and I felt as if my legs had been replaced by wings! On the court, I felt like I could do anything," Patrick says.

In everyday life, he gets around using a wheelchair and occasionally prosthetic legs.

"I never use [my prosthetic legs] for athletic activities. I like the lightness and manoeuvrability* of my competition wheelchair. To me, it means freedom!"

From basketballs to birdies

The skills Richard acquired in basketball, as well as his ease of movement in a wheelchair, helped him make the transition to Para badminton. However, he did have one hurdle.

"I found it hard mastering my swing. In the beginning, my teammates would tease me, saying that I was holding my racquet like a frying pan!" he says with a laugh.

PARA BADMINTON

There are three categories of athletes in Para badminton, which will make its Paralympic Games debut in Tokyo: standing, wheelchair, and short stature. The rules are similar to those for traditional badminton.

Like the wheelchair used in basketball, the one used in badminton is fast, manoeuvrable, and extra stable. But since contact is rare, the badminton chair is lighter and less sturdy, and it does not have bumpers. And the front part of the frame is elongated to allow the athlete to bend over to hit the shuttlecock.

CHANTAL PETITCLERC

Sport: Wheelchair racing

Date of birth:
December 15, 1969

Birthplace: Saint-Marc-des-Carrières, Quebec

Inspired by: The writer Simone de Beauvoir, for her passion and the free way she led her life

Chantal Petitclerc possesses remarkable determination, boundless energy, a positive attitude... and a radiant smile. She has good reason to grin since she has won more medals in Para athletics than any other female athlete of any nationality.

Chantal has taken part in five Paralympic Games (in 1992, 1996, 2000, 2004, and 2008) and reached the podium 21 times!

Chantal also holds many records, including the Canadian track records for all distances from 100 metres to 1500 metres. She is especially proud of the five gold medals she won in 2008 in Beijing, which was where, at 38 years of age, she ended her brilliant athletic career.

THRIVING ON CHALLENGES

Chantal was an active child but not very athletic. At the age of 13, she had an accident when she and a friend were making a bicycle ramp out of a barn door. In a moment that changed her life, the heavy door fell on her and broke her spine. With her legs paralyzed, Chantal had to learn to get around using a wheelchair.

When she returned to school, she would swim during lunch hour on the advice of her phys. ed. teacher.

"Swimming helped me become more independent in a wheelchair by developing my endurance and muscle strength," Chantal says. "It also awakened my spirit of competition."

At 18, Chantal was introduced to Wheelchair racing by Pierre Pomerleau, a coach from Quebec City. A little while later, she took part in a race using a borrowed wheelchair. Although she finished last, she had been bitten by the racing bug!

An Economical Solution

In 1988, Chantal was getting ready to compete again, but she didn't have the thousands of dollars it took to buy a racing wheelchair. No problem! For $400, a friend put one together for her from used parts. Chantal was named Newcomer of the Year and won a brand-new racing wheelchair!

THE EVOLUTION OF RACING WHEELCHAIRS

Today's racing wheelchairs look nothing like the ones used by athletes in the 1948 Wheelchair Games. Those racers competed in their everyday wheelchairs, which were heavy and unwieldy. Thanks to technological progress, today's racing wheelchairs are much more efficient—as Canadian athlete Brent Lakatos, who holds world records in five Para athletics events, can confirm. An engineer, he's been working with a 3D designer to develop prototypes for a faster racing chair. To make it more aerodynamic,* he has incorporated carbon fibre, a light material that can be moulded into any shape.

Brent Lakatos's wheelchair is elongated and has three wheels. By kneeling and leaning forward, the athlete improves his aerodynamics.

A PARALYMPIAN WILL

During her athletic career, Chantal did everything in her power to reach her goals: training intensively, keeping to a strict diet, and enjoying very limited leisure time.

"Being a high-performance athlete definitely requires sacrifices, but since I was passionate about it, I didn't find it hard. I always enjoyed training. I also liked the pressure and the adrenaline rush during races. Before doing competitive sports, I had no idea I had talent and that it would become my passion. If I hadn't taken a chance, I would have missed out on a very exciting career," she says.

Keeping very busy

Although Chantal is no longer competing, she's still involved in organizations that promote sports and healthy lifestyles for young people. And in another amazing achievement, she was appointed a senator by the Canadian government in 2016.

As Chantal explains, "I want to make a difference in children's lives by convincing the government to adopt measures that will improve their physical and mental health."

KATARINA ROXON

Sport: Para swimming

Date of birth: April 5, 1993

Birthplace: Corner Brook, Newfoundland and Labrador

Inspired by: Her role model, the Para swimmer Stephanie Dixon

Katarina Roxon has had an impressive career. At the age of 15, she was the youngest athlete on the Canadian swim team to compete in the Beijing Paralympic Games. Although she didn't get to climb onto the podium in China, Katarina won many medals in international competition in the ensuing years. She was awarded her first Paralympic Medal in 2016 at the Rio de Janeiro Paralympic Games. That gold medal, for the 100-metre breaststroke, is to this day her most beautiful memory of competition.

"It was the culmination of 12 years of intensive training, with a lot of ups and downs. Standing on the podium listening to the Canadian national anthem, I relived those moments: the doubts, the injuries, the tears, but also the encouragement of my friends and family," she recalls with emotion.

An athlete at heart

Katarina was born with a disability. Her left arm is missing below the elbow. That hasn't stopped her from taking part in a wide range of sports: soccer, taekwondo, volleyball, basketball, badminton, golf, track and field, cross-country running, cheerleading, and, of course, swimming!

A FAMILY AFFAIR

Katarina's parents, who are originally from India, moved to Newfoundland and Labrador in 1990. To help their daughter achieve her dream, they became her coaches. Both of her parents, who are physiotherapists by profession, have played a significant role in her sporting career. Her mother taught her the butterfly stroke, and in 2005, her father became her official coach, taking courses and reading dozens of books on nutrition, psychology, training techniques, and more, to fulfill that role to the fullest. Katarina's sister, Miranda, has for a long time been her training partner. She even took a year off university to help Katarina prepare for the London Paralympic Games.

Now that Katarina herself is working as an assistant coach of a swim team, she's inspired by the example of her parents. Things have come full circle!

PEAKS AND VALLEYS

Like all high-performance athletes, Katarina Roxon has had to overcome many hurdles to achieve her goals. The stress of competition can be intense, and she's faced periods of self-doubt when discouragement threatened to take over.

"When I'm having a tough time as a swimmer, I confide in my friends, my teammates, and my family. I'm lucky to have people around me who support me and believe in me," Katarina says.

Training at the elite level can also lead to injuries, which not only cause pain but can force an athlete to bow out of important competitions—another obstacle Katarina knows well.

"I've had injuries that slowed down my progress, but they didn't lessen my love of swimming or divert me from my goals. To me, any experience—good or bad—is an opportunity to learn and improve," Katarina says.

ADAPTING TO CHANGE

Katarina had to adjust when the swimming pool where she trained was closed for an extended time due to the COVID-19 pandemic.

"Since the age of seven, I've never been away from the pool that long," she says. "To keep in shape, I trained in the gym at home. The reopening of the pool was a big day for me. I was finally able to go back to my favourite environment!"

Stephanie Dixon passes the torch

With a record of wins that includes 19 Paralympic medals, 6 medals at the Parapan American Games, and 10 world records, Ontarian Stephanie Dixon—who now lives in Whitehorse, Yukon—is without a doubt one of the best Para swimmers in the world. Retired since 2010, Stephanie was named chef de mission of Team Canada for the 2019 Parapan American Games as well as the upcoming Paralympic Games in Tokyo.

"I'm eager to play that role again in Tokyo, to share my experience with the Canadian athletes and encourage and support them. When I learned that the Games were being postponed, my heart went out to the athletes, but I am confident that with their adaptability and resilience, they'll get through the situation," she says.

AHMAD ZEIVIDAVI

Sport: Goalball

Date of birth: September 3, 1985

Birthplace: Ahvaz, Iran

Inspired by: Terry Fox, a Canadian athlete who, after losing his leg to cancer, ran a Marathon of Hope across Canada to raise money for cancer research and left a lasting legacy

Ahmad Zeividavi is a champion at Goalball, an exciting sport created for people with visual impairments.

"As a child, I dreamed of doing physical activity, but it was complicated since I've been blind since birth," explains Ahmad. "I discovered Goalball when I was 13 and immediately fell in love with it. It made me feel I was in control of my environment. It's a sport that demands a great deal of concentration and agility, and strong team spirit."

Twelve years later, Ahmad began his career as a member of the Canadian national team. The team competed in the 2012 and 2016 Paralympic Games, and though they didn't bring home any medals, they made up for that by taking two bronze medals at the Parapan American Games (one in Toronto, in 2015, and another in Lima, in 2019).

GOALBALL

Goalball is one of only two Paralympic sports that has no equivalent in the Olympic Games. It was introduced as a demonstration sport at the Paralympic Games in Toronto in 1976.

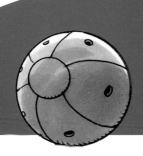

How is Goalball played?

- The object of the game is to score points by rolling the ball into the other team's net, while the opposing players try to block the shots with their bodies. Players at the national and Paralympic levels can shoot the ball as fast as 60 km/h!

- The Goalball court has the same dimensions as a volleyball court. String taped to the floor is used to mark out the playing surface. The players orient themselves by feeling these tactile markings with their hands and feet.

- All players wear opaque eyeshades so that everyone is on an equal footing, whatever their degree of visual impairment.

- The ball contains noise bells so that the athletes can track it. One of the strategies of the game is to roll the ball very gently so that it doesn't make a sound.

A refugee's journey

In 2009, Ahmad left Iran, which was in the throes of a social and economic crisis.

"I fled my country of origin because human rights were not respected there. I decided to settle in Canada, where you can live in freedom and peace. When I landed on Canadian soil, I had no prospects. Through all the hardships, I realized that this country offers great opportunities for success for newcomers, whatever their social status," he says.

In 2016, knowing how difficult it can be to adapt to a new country, Ahmad founded the organization House of Omeed, which assists refugees and new immigrants as they adjust to life in Canada.

QUIET ON THE COURT!

During a Goalball game, the spectators, coaches, and players on the bench have to remain silent so that the players can hear the ball. Of course, when a goal is scored, the spectators are allowed to cheer!

UNFORGETTABLE MOMENTS

Ahmad especially cherishes two incredible Goalball memories. The first was the amazing moment when, at the 2011 IBSA* World Championships and Games, his team defeated the United States, allowing Canada to compete in the London Paralympic Games. And the second was at the Opening Ceremony of those Games, on July 27, 2012, when Ahmad experienced another highlight in his career.

"When I paraded in front of 90,000 spectators at Olympic Stadium in the Canadian athletes' uniform, I was very moved to be representing Canada. This country has done so much for me."

Amy Burk's dogged determination

A native of Prince Edward Island, Amy Burk is one of the highest-scoring Goalball players in the world. Her secret: her exceptional will to win. A member of the national team since 2005, she helped the team win two World Championships (in 2006 and 2011) and take the bronze medal at three Parapan American Games (in 2011, 2015, and 2019).

After playing Goalball for the first time at the age of 13, Amy originally gave up the game, feeling intimidated by its intensity and speed. Luckily for her fans, she came back to it a year later, setting herself a rigorous training regime to develop her skills. Mission accomplished!

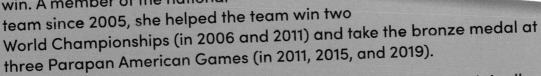

UP-AND-COMING STARS

The next generation of Canadian Para athletes is training vigorously in the hope of competing in the Paralympic Games. Here are four young talents with extremely promising futures.

SANDRINE HAMEL

Date of birth:
August 21, 1997
Birthplace: Montreal, Quebec
Sport: Para snowboard

Sandrine Hamel, who has a spinal malformation and muscle weakness in her right leg, has been snowboarding since the age of eight. She first learned about Para snowboarding when she saw an ad on television featuring a Canadian Para swimmer whose gait was similar to hers, and who was headed to the Rio Paralympic Games. Intrigued, Sandrine checked the list of sports on the Canadian Paralympic Committee's website and saw that Para snowboard was included. A few months later, she took part in her first competitions.

In 2018, the 20-year-old snowboarder joined the national team before placing fifth at the PyeongChang Paralympic Games in both the snowboard cross and banked slalom, an incredible result so early in her career. The following year, she took home a pair of silver medals in both events at the World Championships in Pyhä, Finland.

PUISAND LAI

Date of birth:
July 29, 2000

Birthplace: Honolulu
County, Hawaii

Sport: Wheelchair
basketball

Puisand Lai has used a
wheelchair since the age of
six because her legs are
paralyzed as a result of a
rare disorder. Before falling
in love with Wheelchair
basketball, she participated
in Adaptive sailing, Para ice
hockey, and Wheelchair
tennis. Since taking up
basketball in 2013, she has
become known for her speed
and defensive play.

In 2018, Puisand was chosen
by the national team to
compete in the World
Championships. She was
then the youngest member
of the team, which did very
well, placing fifth. One year
later, the team won the gold
medal at the Lima Parapan
American Games.

WYATT LIGHTFOOT

Date of birth: June 6, 2003

Birthplace: Assiniboia, Saskatchewan

Sport: Para badminton

Wyatt Lightfoot has been playing badminton recreationally since he was four. He also played soccer, volleyball, basketball, and hockey as a child. When he was a preteen, he realized his short stature would prevent him from taking part in certain contact sports (too much risk of injury), but that still left plenty of choice. In 2015, Wyatt started to train to compete in Para badminton.

Wyatt had an especially successful year in 2019. In addition to taking part in the introduction of Para badminton at the Parapan American Games, he was named Junior Para Athlete of the Year by Badminton Canada. Today, he is one of the best Para badminton players in the country. Wyatt hopes to represent Canada in Tokyo when his sport makes its official debut in the Paralympic Games.

MARISSA PAPACONSTANTINOU

Date of birth: October 13, 1999
Birthplace: Toronto, Ontario
Sport: Para athletics (track)

Marissa Papaconstantinou has participated in numerous sports, including soccer, basketball, football, and Para athletics. Born without a right foot, she always especially loved track. But running with an ordinary prosthetic leg was difficult.

At age 12, Marissa got her first running prosthesis, which made it possible for her to develop to her full potential. Just a year later, she broke the Canadian record for the 100-metre sprint.

Marissa, whose specialties are sprinting events (100 metres and 200 metres), took part in her first international competitions in 2015 and competed in the Rio Paralympic Games at the age of 16. She didn't win any medals then, but in 2019, she broke her own Canadian record in the 100-metre sprint at the World Para Athletics Grand Prix in Switzerland.

GLOSSARY

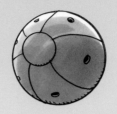

aerodynamic
Designed to move easily through the air

amputate
To surgically remove a limb from the body

competitor
A person who is trying to win or do better than another person

degenerative
Causing the body or part of the body to become weaker or less able to function as time passes

IBSA
The International Blind Sports Federation

manoeuvrability
The quality of being easy to move and direct

Parapan American Games
Related to multisport competitions for Para athletes from 28 countries in the Americas and the Caribbean

persevere
To continue doing something or trying to do something even though it is difficult

physiotherapy
The treatment of a disease or injury with massage, exercises, heat, etc.

prosthesis
An artificial aid or substitute for a missing part of the body (also known as "prosthetic device")

resilience
The ability to become strong, healthy, or successful again after something bad happens

sledge
A metal-framed sled on two skate-like blades used in Para ice hockey

therapeutic
Related to the treatment of disease or injury